O9-AIF-600

# My First Pocket Guide

# Maryland

## By Carole Marsh

Correlates with Maryland's
**CSSS**
Content Standards for Social Studies

THE **MARYLAND** ExperiencE

# The GALLOPADE GANG

Carole Marsh
Bob Longmeyer
Chad Beard
Cecil Anderson
Steven Saint-Laurent
Karin Petersen
Billie Walburn

Doug Boston
Jill Sanders
William Nesbitt, Jr.
Kathy Zimmer
Wanda Coats
Terry Briggs
Jackie Clayton

Pam Dufresne
Cranston Davenport
Lisa Stanley
Antoinette Miller
Victoria DeJoy

Published by GALLOPADE INTERNATIONAL

www.marylandexperience.com
800-536-2GET • www.gallopade.com

**Gallopade is proud to be a member of these educational organizations and associations:**

NSSEA

SHOPA MEMBER
Schools, Home, & Office Products Association

## Other Maryland Experience Products

• The Maryland Experience!
• The BIG Maryland Reproducible Activity Book
• The Maryland Coloring Book
• My First Book About Maryland!
• Maryland "Jography": A Fun Run Through Our State
• Maryland Jeopardy!: Answers and Questions About Our State
• The Maryland Experience! Sticker Pack
• The Maryland Experience! Poster/Map
• Discover Maryland CD-ROM
• Maryland "Geo" Bingo Game
• Maryland "Histo" Bingo Game

Word From the Author... (okay, a few words)...

Hi!
Here's your own handy pocket guide about the great state of Maryland! It really will fit in a pocket—I tested it. And it really will be useful when you want to know a fact you forgot, to bone up for a test, or when your teacher says, "I wonder . . ." and you have the answer—instantly! Wow, I'm impressed!

Get smart, have fun!
Carole Marsh

**Maryland Basics** explores your state's symbols and their special meanings!

**Maryland Geography** digs up the what's where in your state!

**Maryland History** is like traveling through time to some of your state's great moments!

**Maryland People** introduces you to famous personalities and your next-door neighbors!

**Maryland Places** shows you where you might enjoy your next family vacation!

**Maryland Nature** - no preservatives here, just what Mother Nature gave to Maryland!

All the real fun stuff that we just HAD to save for its own section!

Maryland Basics

Maryland Geography

Maryland History

Maryland People

Maryland Places

Maryland Nature

Maryland Miscellany

# Who Named You?

Maryland's official state name is...

# Maryland

**State Name**

**Word Definition**

OFFICIAL: appointed, authorized, or approved by a government or organization

## Statehood: April 28, 1788

Maryland was the 7th state to join the United States.

Maryland was recognized on a state-commemorative quarter in the year 2000. The design includes the state capitol's dome flanked by two White Oak boughs. It reads, "The Old Line State"!

*Coccinella noemnotata* is my name (that's Latin for Lady Bug)! What's YOURS?

# A Name of Royal Proportions!

When King Charles I issued a charter to Lord Baltimore, he requested the colony be named in honor of his beloved wife, Henrietta Maria. Lord Baltimore honored the request, naming the new colony Maryland.

Queen Henrietta Maria lived from 1609 until 1669. She was the daughter of King Henry IV of France and Marie de Medicis. When she was 16, she married Charles. Because she was Roman Catholic and the English belonged to another church, many people did not trust Henrietta Maria. This made them not trust her husband, either. King Charles was forced to go to the Netherlands. Henrietta Maria returned to France, where she worked hard to help her king. She even sold her jewels to aid in his release. However, King Charles was beheaded!

After Charles' death, the heartbroken queen lived in a Paris convent. She returned to England when her son, Charles II, became king of England in 1660. Henrietta Maria returned to her homeland in 1665 where she lived until her death.

## What's In A Name?

Maryland is not the only name by which our state is recognized. Like many other states, Maryland has some nicknames!

**State Nicknames**

# The Old Line State
# The Free State

During the Revolutionary War Battle of Long Island, stubborn Maryland soldiers distracted the British while General George Washington and his troops escaped to Manhattan. Maryland came to be known as the Old Line State because of those soldiers in the Continental Line.

Maryland is also known as the Pine Tree State.

## State Capital:
# Annapolis

State
Capital/
Capitol

Maryland's first capital was St. Mary's, but in 1694, the capital was moved to Anne Arundel Town. The city's name was soon changed to Annapolis. Annapolis means "City of Anne," and was named in honor of England's Princess Anne.

Maryland's capitol is on a circular street in the center of Annapolis. The site has an interesting history. Three capitol buildings have stood on the same spot. The first, built in 1698, was damaged when lightning struck it and caused a fire that also killed a member of the House of Delegates. The damage was repaired, but in 1704, another fire destroyed it completely. In 1707, a new one was built, but people thought it was so ugly that the General Assembly voted to tear it down! A beautiful new building, still in use today, replaced it.

Word
Definition

CAPITAL: a town or city that is the official seat of government
CAPITOL: the building in which the government officials meet

# State Government

# Who's in Charge Here?

Maryland's GOVERNMENT has three branche

```
                    ┌──────────┼──────────┐
              LEGISLATIVE   EXECUTIVE    JUDICIAL
```

**State Government**

*The legislative branch is called the General Assembly.*

| | | |
|---|---|---|
| Two Houses: The Senate (47 members); House of Delegates (141 members) | A governor, a lieutenant governor, an attorney general, and a comptroller of the treasury | Court of appeals (7 justices), court of special appeals, circuit courts, and district courts |

Of Maryland's 23 counties, 15 are governed by boards of county commissioners. The other eight are governed by county councils. The city of Baltimore has its own government, independent from any county.

When you are 18 and register to vote according to Maryland laws, you can vote! Please do so! Your vote counts!

State Flag

*Maryland's state flag was adopted in 1904.*

It is divided into four equal sections with the top left and bottom right quadrants bearing the gold-and-black coat of arms of the Calverts, who initially claimed the state for England. The top right and bottom left quadrants contain the red-and-white coat of arms of the Crosslands, which was the family of the first Lord Baltimore's mother.

Maryland has a law that says if the state flag is attached to a flagpole, the only ornament allowed on the top of the flagstaff is a gold cross bottony.

Maryland's state flag was first flown on October 11, 1880 in a Baltimore parade to mark the city's 150th birthday!

# State Seal

Maryland's state seal was adopted in 1876. It has remained the same since. Maryland received its first Great Seal shortly after the colony was settled in the 1630s. In the center, a shield shows the colors of the Calvert (black and gold) and the Crossland (red and white) families. To the left of the shield stands a man with a shovel, to the right stands a fisherman. The background of the seal is in royal blue, surrounded by a gold border. The governor and the secretary of state use the state seal to authenticate laws passed by the General Assembly. It's also used for other official purposes. The secretary of state is the "official keeper of the seal."

**State Seal & Motto**

**Word Definition**

MOTTO: a sentence, phrase, or word expressing the spirit or purpose of an organization or group

# State Motto

*Maryland's state motto is...*

*Fatti maschii parole femine*

This is Italian for "Manly deeds, womanly words." This motto is actually the motto of the founding family of Maryland, the Calverts.

The state seal is on a lot of government buildings in Maryland.

10

# Baltimore Oriole

The Baltimore Oriole is also known as the Northern Oriole. Another name for it is the Hang-nest because together the male and female build a nest that looks like a pouch hanging from the trees.

The males are known for their bright colors—a bright orange chest with orange in the tail while the wings are black with white bars. The female is colorful too, just a little duller than the male. She's mainly olive and yellowish with white wing bars.

The Maryland legislature passed a law protecting the Baltimore Oriole in 1882. The bird is also mentioned on the state's Nongame and Endangered Species Conservation Act of 1975. Scientists think the Oriole population is decreasing because they eat insects that may have been poisoned by insecticides.

Baltimore also has a professional baseball team called the Baltimore Orioles.

State
Tree

*Tall oaks from little acorns grow.*
—David Everett

## WHITE OAK

The White Oak is probably the best known of all the Oak trees. Its beauty caught the eye of early colonists in New England and mid-Atlantic states like Maryland.

While White Oaks are valuable for shade and shelter, the Indians used their fruit, the acorn, as food. Today, the Maryland state tree is also valued for its beautiful, strong lumber. It is used to make furniture, boats, and barrels.

# BLACK-EYED SUSAN

*And parting summer's lingering bloom delay'd.*

—Oliver Goldsmith

**State Flower and Insect**

Black-eyed Susans are actually daisies or coneflowers and are members of the sunflower family. They grow in the area east of the Mississippi River. They get their name from the dark brown center in the middle of their slender golden petals. They grow 2 to 3 feet (61 to 91.4 centimeters) in height. These flowers bloom between May and August, usually in fields or along the roadside.

# BALTIMORE CHECKERSPOT BUTTERFLY

With a name like the Baltimore Checkerspot, it certainly seemed logical to make this butterfly the Maryland state insect in 1973. Baltimore Checkerspots pollinate plants as they move from one to another in search of food. Their dark wings are edged with spots of white and orange. They have distinctive knobs on the ends of their antennae.

## Chesapeake Bay Retriever

The Chesapeake Bay Retriever is one of few breeds developed in the United States. They were bred to be hunting dogs—mainly to recover ducks and other waterfowl for hunters.

**State Dog**

According to legend, these dogs were descendants of two Newfoundland dogs that survived a British shipwreck off the Maryland coast. When the Newfoundlands were bred with Maryland coonhounds, the result was the Chesapeake Bay Retriever!

Chesapeake Bay Retrievers are versatile, intelligent, and strong. They're used as service dogs by law enforcement agencies. They also make great rescue dogs. Because they're loyal and gentle, they're a favorite visitor at nursing homes and hospitals in pet therapy programs. The American Kennel Club registered the first Chesapeake Bay Retriever in 1878. It became the state dog in 1964.

RIDDLE: What do you get when you cross the Maryland state flower with the state dog?

A black-eyed dog that retrieves Susans from the Chesapeake Bay!

# The Diamondback Terrapin

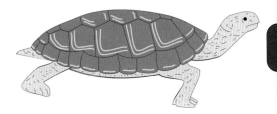

State
Reptile

This reptile was named for the diamond-shaped rings on its upper shell. They will only live in unpolluted saltwater marshes and rivers. When they're around, Marylanders know their wetlands are healthy. Diamondbacks spend the Winter hibernating underwater in the mud. In late May, they come out to mate, nest, and sun themselves on beaches and sand dunes.

Terrapins are always turtles, but not all turtles are terrapins!

Settlers relied heavily on the Diamondback Terrapin for food. The Indians taught the colonists how to roast the turtles in hot coals. They became a delicacy, especially when served in a stew with cream and sherry. However, they were harvested until they were almost extinct, so laws were made to protect them.

15

# State Dinosaur

## Astrodon johnstoni

Maryland's state dinosaur is the *Astrodon johnstoni*. Philip Tyson found two unusual teeth near Muirkirk in 1858. Tyson was the State Agricultural Chemist when he made one of the first dinosaur discoveries in the nation. He gave the teeth to a dentist, Dr. Christopher Johnston, who sliced one in half and found it to be star-shaped. *Astrodon* means "star tooth," and *johnstoni* is in recognition of the dentist's revelation.

*Astrodons* lived in Maryland millions of years ago. They were sauropods or lizard-hips, who looked a little like brontosaurs. These plant-eaters weighed up to 20 tons (18.2 metric tons). They grew to be 50 to 60 feet (15.2 to 18.3 meters) long and stood 30 feet (9.1 meters) tall.

**State Dinosaur**

# State Fossil Shell & State Crustacean

## State Fossil Shell

The Maryland **State Fossil Shell** is the *Ecphora gardnerae gardnerae* (Wilson). It housed an extinct snail that lived in the Chesapeake Bay and other Atlantic coastal waters. This snail lived nearly 3 million years ago. The fossils have been found in the Calvert Cliffs in Calvert County and Chancellor Point in St. Mary's County. Its name comes from the Greek word *ekphora*, which means "protruding." *Gardnerae* is in honor of paleontologist Julia Gardner, and Wilson came from the man who gave the species its name.

**State Fossil Shell & State Crustacean**

## State Crustacean

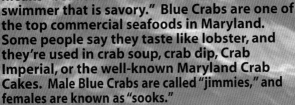

Maryland named the Blue Crab its state crustacean in 1989. The crab's Latin name, *Callinectes sapidus*, means "beautiful swimmer that is savory." Blue Crabs are one of the top commercial seafoods in Maryland. Some people say they taste like lobster, and they're used in crab soup, crab dip, Crab Imperial, or the well-known Maryland Crab Cakes. Male Blue Crabs are called "jimmies," and females are known as "sooks."

# Milk

In 1998, Milk was named the official state beverage of Maryland. The nutritious beverage is easily accessible—in 1999 there were 85,000 dairy cows in the state. Most of these are Holsteins. Their white hide with large black splotches makes them easy to spot. Frederick and Wilson counties have the most dairy cows.

**State Beverage**

## Maryland Milk Shake

Take 2 scoops of vanilla ice cream, 1 cup of milk, and blend in a blender with 2 tablespoons of peanut butter!

# Jousting

Maryland is one of the few states with an official state sport. In 1962 Marylanders chose the majestic sport of jousting as the state sport. Jousting's popularity goes back to Maryland's early colonial period. After the Civil War, it became even more popular. Men, women, and even children participate. Contestants and spectators often dress in medieval costumes to revive the pageantry of the time when the games began. Competitors are even called "knights" and "maids."

**State Sport**

Maryland jousters compete in "ring tournaments." They charge their horses at full-gallop through an 80-yard (73.2-meter) course. Using a long, sharp-tipped lance, they try to spear rings suspended from a stand. Riders have 8 seconds to complete the course, and score points for each ring they spear. Some of the rings are as small as ¼ inch (0.64 centimeters) in diameter!

19

## Striped Bass (Rockfish)

**State Fish & State Boat**

Maryland's wealth of waterways also means a wealth of fish. In 1965, the Maryland lawmakers decreed that the Striped Bass (Rockfish) would be the state fish. They described it as "the abundant and unexcelled delicacy of the Chesapeake Bay." The Rockfish is known for being a challenge to sports fishermen, as well as being good to eat. The biggest Maryland Rockfish was caught in 1995 in the Chesapeake Bay, and weighed 67 pounds, 8 ounces (30.4 kilograms).

## Skipjack

Maryland's state boat could probably be used to haul in the state fish, but they're more commonly used to dredge oysters from Chesapeake Bay. Skipjacks are the last boats under sails in America to be used for working purposes. Today they're used more often for tourists than fishing, though. They were developed in the 1890s and named for skipjack fish. Skipjack is a term used to describe fish that leap in and out of the water. Skipjacks have a reputation for being fast. Today the number of Skipjack boats has sharply declined and efforts are being made to preserve them.

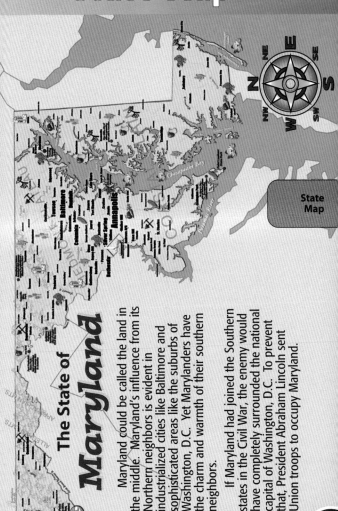

## The State of Maryland

Maryland could be called the land in the middle. Maryland's influence from its Northern neighbors is evident in industrialized cities like Baltimore and sophisticated areas like the suburbs of Washington, D.C. Yet Marylanders have the charm and warmth of their southern neighbors.

If Maryland had joined the Southern states in the Civil War, the enemy would have completely surrounded the national capital of Washington, D.C. To prevent that, President Abraham Lincoln sent Union troops to occupy Maryland.

# State Location

Maryland is located on America's Eastern Seaboard between Pennsylvania and Virginia.

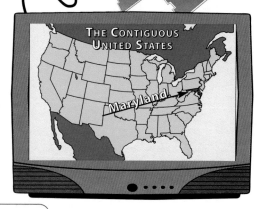

THE CONTIGUOUS UNITED STATES

Maryland

Word Definition

LATITUDE: Imaginary lines which run horizontally east and west around the globe
LONGITUDE: Imaginary lines which run vertically north and south around the globe

# State Neighbors

## ON THE BORDER!

### These border Maryland:

**States:** Virginia     West Virginia
           Delaware     Pennsylvania
**Bodies of water:**     Atlantic Ocean
                    Chesapeake Bay

State Neighbors

In 1791, Maryland supplied nearly
70 square miles (181 square kilometers) of land to help
establish a national capital— Washington, D.C.

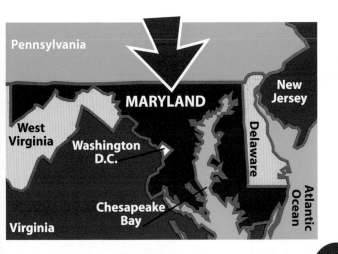

# I'll Take the Low Road...

Maryland is 238 miles (383 kilometers) from east to west...or west to east. Either way, it's a long walk—from Oakland to Ocean City or Ocean City to Oakland!

**East-West North-South Area**

**Total Area: 12,297 square miles (31,847 square kilometers)**
**Land Area: 10,460 square miles (27,089 square kilometers)**

Maryland is 124 miles (200 kilometers) from north to south...or south to north. Either way, it's still a long walk—from Liberty Grove to Lawsonia or Lawsonia to Liberty Grove!

Maryland has the narrowest width of any state. Near Hancock, it is only 1 mile (1.61 kilometers) wide!

This is a compass rose. It helps you find the right direction on a map!

## HIGHEST POINT
Backbone Mountain—3,360 feet (1,024 meters) above sea level

Highest &
Lowest
Points

Hoye Crest is the highest point of Backbone Mountain. It's named in honor of Captain Charles Edward Hoye.

Captain Hoye was a decorated veteran, serving in both the Spanish-American War and World War I. Following his military career, he went to the Philippines and taught for 25 years. He returned home to Garrett County, Maryland, after he retired, and worked to preserve the local history by founding the Garrett County Historical Society.

On Labor Day 1952, Governor Theodore McKeldin dedicated Maryland's high point as Hoye Crest as a tribute to one of Garrett County's favorite sons.

## LOWEST POINT
Sea level along the Atlantic Ocean coastline

# I'm County-ing on You!

Maryland is divided into 23 counties.

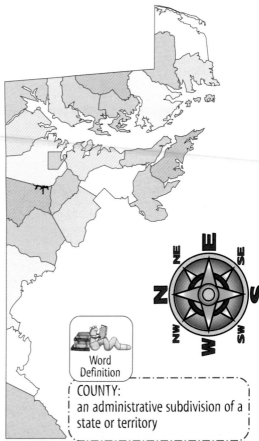

State
Counties

This is the top of Maryland!

Word
Definition

COUNTY:
an administrative subdivision of a
state or territory

# Natural Resources

## It's All Natural!

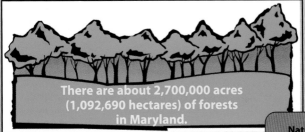

There are about 2,700,000 acres (1,092,690 hectares) of forests in Maryland.

Word Definition

NATURAL RESOURCES: things that exist in or are formed by nature

**Minerals:**
STONE
MARBLE
COAL
SAND
GRAVEL
LIMESTONE
OYSTER SHELL
SANDSTONE
MARBLE
GRANITE

Seafood is a major natural resource of Maryland, especially the blue crab and oysters.

# Weather

## Weather, Or Not?!

In general, Maryland has a pleasant climate—not too hot or too cold.

Sometimes in late Summer during hurricane season, tropical storms hit the coast. They uproot trees, destroy property, and even injure or kill people.

**Weather**

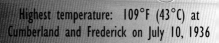

Highest temperature: 109°F (43°C) at Cumberland and Frederick on July 10, 1936

°F=Degrees Fahrenheit °C=Degrees Celsius

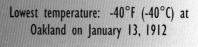

Lowest temperature: -40°F (-40°C) at Oakland on January 13, 1912

Hurricane Agnes struck Maryland in 1972, doing millions of dollars' worth of damage.

# Topography

## BACK ON TOP

Maryland's topography varies from the flat coastline on the east to the mountainous regions in the west. Sloping hills called the piedmont area make up the region between the coast and the mountains.

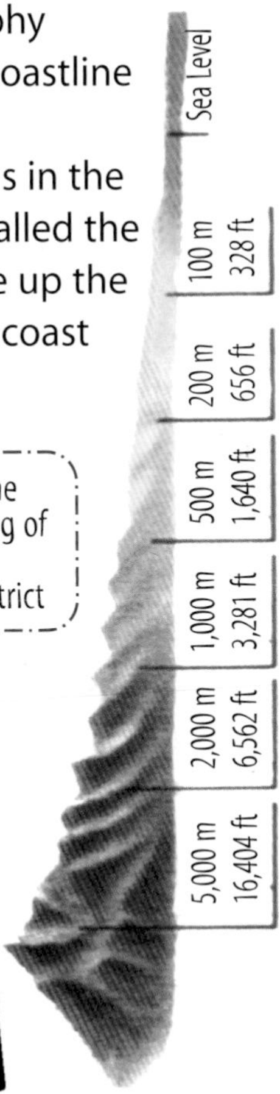

| Word Definition | TOPOGRAPHY: the detailed mapping of the features of a small area or district |

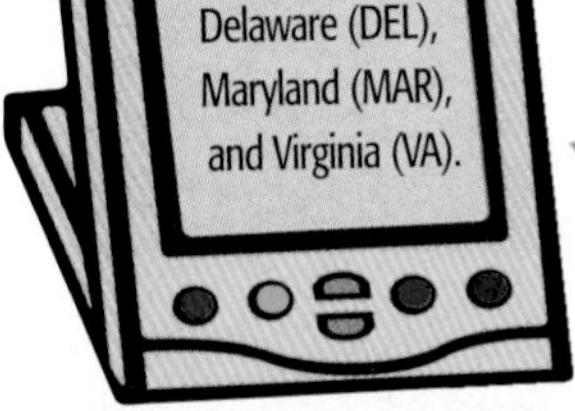

Sea Level

100 m — 328 ft

200 m — 656 ft

500 m — 1,640 ft

1,000 m — 3,281 ft

2,000 m — 6,562 ft

5,000 m — 16,404 ft

Three states make up the Delmarva Peninsula: Delaware (DEL), Maryland (MAR), and Virginia (VA).

# King of the Hill

## *Mountains*

South Mountain
Quirauk Mountain
Backbone Mountain
Green Ridge Mountain
Great Savage Mountain
Meadow Mountain
Negro Mountain
Sugar Loaf Mountain

## *Ranges*

Appalachian
Allegheny
Blue Ridge
Catoctin

On top of Old Smoky...

# Major Rivers

## A River Runs Through It!

Maryland's waterways are important to the state for industry, transportation, and even for determining the state's borders. Many of Maryland's rivers flow into the Chesapeake Bay. The Potomac forms the boundary between Maryland and West Virginia and Virginia. The Youghiogheny and others flow from the Appalachian Plateau westward until they join the Ohio River.

The Chesapeake Bay is nicknamed the "Gateway to the Sea." It's the largest inlet along the Atlantic coast.

Major Rivers

Here are some of Maryland's major rivers:

- Potomac
- Susquehanna
- Severn
- Gunpowder
- Patapsco
- Chester
- Choptank
- Nanticoke
- Pocomoke
- Youghiogheny

# Gone Fishin'

**Despite all the rivers and streams in Maryland, there are no large natural lakes. Almost all the lakes in Maryland are man-made!**

**Here are a few of Maryland's reservoirs**

**Deep Creek Lake**

**Triadelphia Reservoir**

**Pretty Boy Reservoir**

**Liberty Lake**

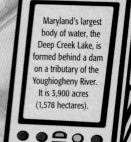

Maryland's largest body of water, the Deep Creek Lake, is formed behind a dam on a tributary of the Youghiogheny River. It is 3,900 acres (1,578 hectares).

Word Definition

RESERVOIR: a body of water stored for public use

# ARE YOU A CITY MOUSE... OR COUNTRY MOUSE?

Have you heard these wonderful Maryland city, town, and crossroad names? Perhaps you can start your own list!

**Cities & Towns**

LARGER TOWNS:
Baltimore
Rockville
Hagerstown
Bowie
Annapolis
Frederick
Gaithersburg
Cumberland
College Park
Salisbury
Takoma Park

OTHER TOWNS:
Accident
American Corner
Bivalve
Boring
Chase
Chance
Flintstone
Friendship
Girdletree
Good Luck
Issue
Level
Rising Sun
Welcome

Welcome to Rising Sun, an American Corner in the great state of Maryland. It's never Boring when there's a Chance you may get into a Chase and have an Accident, but it's not a big Issue. We wish you Friendship and Good Luck!

33

## Major Interstate Highways

I-68, I-70, I-81, I-83, I-95, I-97, I-270

Maryland has more than 27,400 miles (44,095 kilometers) of roadways.

Transpor-
tation

## Railroads

The Baltimore and Ohio Railroad was the first to serve as both a passenger and freight line. About 1,000 miles (1,609 kilometers) of track run through Maryland.

## Major Airports

The largest of Maryland's 135 airports is the Baltimore-Washington International Airport located in Friendship, a suburb of Baltimore.

## Ports

Maryland has three major ports at Cambridge, Baltimore, and Annapolis. All three face the Chesapeake Bay. Maryland's 31 miles (50 kilometers) of coastline along the Atlantic Ocean cannot be used for commercial ports, mainly because of the barrier islands that lie along the coast.

# Timeline

|  |  |
|------|-------|
| 1608 | Captain John Smith sails into Chesapeake Bay |
| 1632 | Cecil Calvert, Lord Baltimore, receives charter from England's King Charles I |
| 1633 | Cecil's brother, Leonard, is named governor of Maryland region |
| 1634 | Governor Calvert and colonists found St. Mary's City |
| 1652 | Maryland receives upper Chesapeake Bay in treaty from Susquehannock Indians |
| 1654 | Virginia Puritans led by William Claiborne take over Maryland |
| 1658 | Leonard Calvert regains control of Maryland |
| 1765 | Stamp Act results in riots in Annapolis |
| 1776 | Maryland declares independence from England |
| 1784 | Congress ratifies Treaty of Paris in Annapolis |
| 1788 | Maryland becomes 7th state |
| 1813 | British blockade Chesapeake Bay |
| 1861 | Marylanders attack Union forces at Baltimore |
| 1862 | Union forces declare victory at Antietam |
| 1978 | Camp David peace accords signal end of fighting between Egypt and Israel |
| 1999 | Celebration 350 marks 350th anniversary of the founding of Annapolis |

Timeline

In 1767, Charles Mason and Jeremiah Dixon mapped the boundary between Maryland and Pennsylvania. It became known as the famous Mason-Dixon Line.

# Here come the humans!

Thousands of years ago, nomadic hunters came to the area that would one day become the state of Maryland. They were in search of deer and other wild game. These Paleo-Indians were descended from people who crossed the Bering Strait between Asia and Alaska. They became the ancestors of Maryland's Native American population.

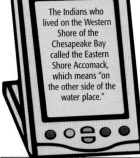

The Indians who lived on the Western Shore of the Chesapeake Bay called the Eastern Shore Accomack, which means "on the other side of the water place."

# Early Indians

Maryland's early Indians soon organized into tribal territories. The Pocomoke, Choptank, and Nanticoke lived on the Eastern Shore. In southern Maryland, the Anaco, Piscataway, Yaocomaco, and Patuxent were a part of the Algonquian tribes. These tribes were separate, but spoke a similar language and had similar customs.

The tribes were usually small—only a few hundred in number. Families built wigwams of saplings covered with marsh grasses. The women grew corn, tobacco, beans, and squash, while the men hunted and fished. The tribes often ate oysters and large mounds of discarded oysters shells, known as midden heaps, could be found years after villages were abandoned.

**Early Indians**

The Susquehannock were a powerful tribe that lived to the north along the river that bears their name. They were very tall and strong and dominated the neighboring tribes to the south!

Word Definition

WAMPUM: beads, pierced and strung, used by Indians as money, or for ornaments or ceremonies.

# Exploration

It's not known for sure when European explorers first came to Maryland, but historians believe French, Italian, and Spanish explorers arrived in the early 1500s looking for furs and Christian converts.

Captain John Smith and a party of English colonists sailed into the Chesapeake Bay in 1608. They were greeted by a band of Susquehannock Indians who honored their arrival with gifts of furs, arrows, and tobacco pipes.

**Exploration**

Only about 3,000 Indians lived in Maryland when the European explorers arrived.

Fur traders from the English colony of Virginia also came to Maryland. They were hoping to trade goods with the Indians.

# Colonization

## Home, Sweet, Home

In 1632, George Calvert, the first Lord Baltimore, asked King Charles I of England for a charter to colonize the land north of the Potomac River, which had been part of the Virginia colony. He wanted to create a colony where Catholics and Protestants could live, work, and freely worship God. The request was granted, but after Lord Baltimore died. The charter

was given to his son Cecil Calvert, the second Lord Baltimore, who organized an expedition of 200 colonists bound for the New World.

Colonization

Late in 1633, the colonists sailed from England on the *Ark* and the *Dove* under the leadership of Cecil's younger brother, Leonard Calvert, who served as provincial governor of Maryland. In March 1634, the expedition landed at St. Clements Island. They established St. Mary's City at the site of a former Yaocomaco Indian village, which they bought from the tribe. Father Andrew White, a Jesuit priest, recorded the venture for posterity.

In 1689, Protestants overthrew the Calvert government and demanded direct rule by the British Crown. In 1715, the Calverts once again regained control.

**William Claiborne, who founded the first European settlement on Kent Island, refused to accept Lord Calvert's authority. In 1654, Claiborne seized the Maryland Colony and governed it until 1658 when Calvert regained control.**

# Oyster Wars

In the 1800s, everyone wanted the delicious oysters that came from Chesapeake Bay. In the 1820s, commercial canning was developed in Baltimore, which enabled oysters to be preserved for shipping. A law issued in 1865 allowed fishermen to harvest oysters by dragging the bottom of the bay with weighted nets or dredges, instead of "tonging" them with long, scissor-like tongs. This new method significantly increased the daily oyster catch.

Outsiders were very eager to make money in the profitable oyster business. In the 1870s, '80s, and '90s, pirate dredgers from Virginia sneaked in, but Maryland was ready for them! An "Oyster Navy" was created, and several armed boats patrolled the Maryland side of Chesapeake Bay.

**Oyster Wars**

During those 30 years, the famous "Oyster Wars" claimed dozens of lives, and made headlines in newspapers all across the country.

The largest natural oyster bed in the world is said to be the Swan Point Bar, located off Rock Hall.

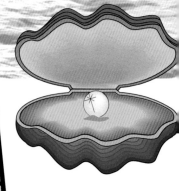

# Fact Or Fiction?

● According to the wise and weather-worn watermen, during a waning moon is the best time to eat hard crabs—that's when they have the most meat. Soft crabs are tastiest and most plentiful when the moon is full!

● As the story goes, a Union soldier was traveling through Maryland on his way home from the Civil War. He stopped to spend the night at an inn in Allegany County, where he was robbed and murdered. In his attempt to escape, he laid a bleeding hand on a door and left a bloody handprint. To this day, no one has ever been able to remove the blood-red stain.

Legends & Lore

If you've been to Dorchester County, you may have heard the old superstition that says it's a very good thing to sing while you're catching oysters. *La La La La La!*

41

# Freedom!

Colonists began to resent the strong-handed rule of royal governors. They objected to paying taxes to a British motherland that was no longer their homeland. Britain thought the colonies would be a good place to find some cash to replenish the treasury after the Seven Years War!

**Revolution**

In October 1774, the brig *Peggy Stewart* anchored in Annapolis Harbor, loaded with tax-paid British tea. A group of patriots wanted to keep the tea from coming ashore and threatened the ship's owner, Anthony Stewart, and his family. To satisfy the crowd, Stewart didn't just burn the tea—he set fire to the whole ship and watched it burn down to the waterline!

The American Revolution started in 1775. Many Marylanders fought bravely. The colonists continued tirelessly and courageously year after year. England finally surrendered in 1781 at Yorktown, Virginia. In 1784, Congress met in Maryland's State House in Annapolis to ratify the Treaty of Paris, officially ending the Revolutionary War. The United States of America was born!

British ships blockaded Chesapeake Bay. Baltimore merchants armed their boats, sent them out as "privateers," and captured hundreds of British ships.

# Slaves and Slavery

## OF HUMAN BONDAGE

The issue of slavery divided Maryland. The small farmers in the western region never used slaves, but the tobacco planters of the Coastal Plain region depended on them to tend and grow their crops.

Thousands of slaves were brought from Africa to America. Long days, hard labor, disease, and bad weather made plantation life miserable. Slaves could be sold and their families divided at any time by their owners.

Many slaves shared unique talents, such as creating favorite foods we enjoy today. They also fought for their freedom in creative ways. Slave women created quilts with secret designs which helped many find their way along the Underground Railroad, a secret system of "stations" where escaped slaves could find shelter and eventually reach freedom in the North. They were escorted from station to station by folks who disapproved of slavery and believed everyone had the right to be free!

Word Definition

ABOLITIONIST: person who believed slavery was wrong and should be abolished.

# The Civil War

## Brother

The Civil War was fought over slavery and states' rights. Southern states, with plantations and slaves, were on one side of this battle. Northern states, who opposed slavery or had no need for it, were on the other side. Some states remained neutral on the issue.

Maryland's loyalty was divided between the North and the South. On April 19, 1861, the first blood of the war was shed in Baltimore when Marylanders attacked Union troops as they were changing trains headed for Washington, D.C. By the end of the war, more than 50,000 Marylanders had fought for the Union and about 20,000 sided with the Confederacy.

President Abraham Lincoln, recognizing its strategic importance to the Union, ordered federal troops to occupy Maryland. Any attempts to secede from (leave) the Union were thwarted—sometimes by military force!

The devastating Battle of Antietam was fought on September 17, 1862 near the town of Sharpsburg. At Antietam Creek, 41,000 Confederate soldiers fought 87,000 Union troops. More than 4,700 soldiers were killed, more than 18,000 wounded, and 3,000 were missing in action. The Battle of Antietam was the bloodiest single day of fighting in American history!

# The Civil War

## vs. Brother

The Civil War was also called the War Between the States. Soldiers often found themselves fighting against former friends and neighbors, even brother against brother. Those who did survive often went home without an arm, leg, or both, since amputation was the "cure" for most battlefield wounds. More Americans were killed during the Civil War than during World Wars I and II together!

**The Civil War**

In 1863, the Emancipation Proclamation, issued by U.S. president Abraham Lincoln, freed the slaves still under Confederate control. Some slaves became sharecroppers; others went to Northern states to work in factories.

# Get It In Writing!

English Charter for Maryland region, 1632
issued by King Charles I

Susquehannock Treaty, 1652
cedes Indian land on upper Chesapeake Bay to Maryland

First state constitution, 1776
Maryland declares its independence from England

Maryland ratifies U.S. Constitution, 1788

New state constitution, 1864
abolishes slavery

Current state constitution, 1867

# Immigrants

# WELCOME TO AMERICA!

People have come to Maryland from other states and countries around the world. As time goes by, the state's population grows more diverse. This means that people of different races and from different cultures and ethnic backgrounds have moved to Maryland.

Early residents originally came from England, Ireland, Scotland, and Germany. More recently, people have come from Russia, Poland, Greece, and other European countries. Marylanders are very proud of their ethnic heritages! Maryland's population also includes Hispanics, Asians, Pacific Islanders, Native Americans, African-Americans, and people from many other cultures.

**Immigrants**

Baltimore has often been called the "City of Neighborhoods" because it's home to many different ethnic groups. Every September, during the annual City Fair, Baltimore celebrates its cultural diversity with concerts, food, and other fun festivities!

# Disasters & Catastrophes

## 1785

A tremendous gale of wind known as a northeaster strikes Chesapeake Bay; rages for three days; drives more than 30 ships ashore

## 1873

A fire starts near the boiler room on the steamboat *Wawaset*; the fire destroys the steamer and kills 76 people as the *Wawaset* sails down the Potomac River

**Disasters & Catastrophes**

## 1877

Ten people die during the Baltimore and Ohio (B & O) Railroad strikes and riots over reductions in wages; strikes cripple railway service across the country; strikes end when federal troops are brought in

## 1904

Devastating fire roars through Baltimore

## 1963

Pan Am Flight 214 is struck by lightning; crashes near Elkton, killing all 81 passengers and crew on board

Lightning often strikes planes, runs from wing to wing or nose to tail, and discharges into the air. Planes now have radar systems on board that track approaching storms!

# Legal Stuff

## 1649
Toleration Act passes; grants religious freedom

## 1826
Jews receive the right to vote

## 1902
Maryland becomes first state to pass a workmen's compensation law

## 1935
Thurgood Marshall argues case for the National Association for the Advancement of Colored People that opens doors of the University of Maryland Law School to African-Americans

## 1961
Maryland becomes first state to create a public agency for historic preservation

# Women & Children

## 1826
Legislature provides for the creation of public schools

## 1881
Charity Organization Society is founded in Baltimore to eliminate child labor, improve education, raise money for scholarships, and open neighborhood houses for recreation and classes

Women & Children

## 1920
Women gain suffrage nationally through the 19th Amendment

## 1937
Lillie Mae Capel Flowers becomes the first woman in the U.S. to be licensed to operate a commercial power vessel on rivers, bays, or oceans

## 1940
D'Arcy Grant, captain of the schooner *Fannie Insley*, is the only female skipper of a freight-hauling ship on the Chesapeake Bay

# Fight! Fight! Fight!

Wars that had an impact on Maryland:

- **French and Indian War**
- **Seven Years War**
- **American Revolution**
- **War of 1812**
- **Mexican-American**
- **Civil War**
- **World War I**
- **World War II**
- **Korean War**
- **Vietnam War**
- **Persian Gulf War**

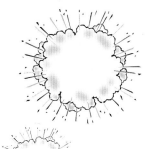

Wars

51

# Oh! Say, Can You See

In September 1814, Francis Scott Key, a Maryland-born lawyer, boarded a British vessel in the Baltimore harbor to bargain for the release of an American prisoner. Fearful Key would reveal their battle plans to the Americans, the British held him captive. He watched as the British attacked Fort McHenry—battling the Americans for 24 hours.

From the ship's deck, Key strained through the smoke and haze of the battle to see what was left of the fort. As dawn broke, Key was overcome with joy when he saw the U.S. flag waving proudly. He knew the Americans had won!

Inspired by the sight, Key wrote a song that was to become the national anthem—"The Star-Spangled Banner"! Americans still stand proudly to sing the familiar song:

*Oh! say, can you see, by the dawn's early light,*
*What so proudly we hailed at the twilight's last gleaming,*
*Whose broad stripes and bright stars through the perilous fight*
*Over the ramparts we watched were so gallantly streaming?*
*And the rockets red glare, the bombs bursting in air,*
*Gave proof through the night that our flag was still there…*

The flag that flew over Fort McHenry was the largest U.S. battle flag ever flown! It measured 30 by 42 feet (9 by 13 meters), and was handmade by Mary Young Pickersgill of Baltimore. Today, the flag hangs in the Smithsonian Institution in Washington, D.C.

# Indian Tribes

- Pocomoke
- Choptank
- Nanticoke
- Anaco
- Piscataway
- Yaocomaco
- Patuxent
- Susquehannock

Burial sites and artifacts, such as pottery and axeheads, discovered on the upper Chesapeake Bay show that Indians lived in that area and the surrounding lands for many centuries.

Nearly all Indians left Maryland to escape the settlers. Those who stayed were killed during conflicts with settlers or other Indians, or died of diseases brought by the Europeans. By the late 1700s, almost all of the Indians were gone.

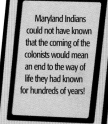

Maryland Indians could not have known that the coming of the colonists would mean an end to the way of life they had known for hundreds of years!

53

# HERE, THERE, EVERYWHERE!

According to legend, the Irish Saint Brendan may have been the first European to see the Chesapeake Bay way back in the 700s.

Thorfinn Karlsefni, a Viking, may have sailed into Chesapeake Bay when he explored the east coast of North America in the 11th century.

John Cabot, from England, may have explored Chesapeake Bay in 1498 on a mission for King Henry VII.

Explorers

Giovanni da Verrazano was an Italian explorer believed to have visited Chesapeake Bay in the 1520s.

Spanish explorers came to the Chesapeake Bay area in the 1520s and later in the 1570s and 1580s.

Captain John Smith explored Chesapeake Bay in 1608.

# State Founders

## Founding Fathers

These people played especially
important roles in early Maryland!

The Calverts—George, Cecil, Charles,
Leonard, Benedict, Charles (another
one), and Frederick were founding
fathers of the state of Maryland. From
George, the first Lord Baltimore who requested the
charter, to Frederick, the last Lord Baltimore—all
played important roles in establishing the great state
of Maryland.

Francis Makemie founded the Presbyterian
Church in America. He built the Rehobeth
Presbyterian Church in 1705 in Somerset County. It's
still the oldest Presbyterian church and congregation
in the U.S.

## Founding Mothers

State
Founders

Margaret Brent may be America's first
"women's libber." She and her siblings
came from England in 1638, and settled in St.
Mary's. Margaret brought papers granting
her the right to hold land—just like the
earliest settlers. Her grant was recorded and
Margaret became the first woman to hold
land in Maryland in her own right.

Elizabeth Ann Seton in 1975, became the first
native-born North American to be canonized by
the Roman Catholic Church. She founded the Sisters
of Charity of St. Vincent de Paul in 1809, and
established schools to help poor and underprivileged
children.

**Harriet Tubman** was born a slave in Bucktown. She risked her life to help more than 300 slaves, including her own parents, escape to freedom on the Underground Railroad! None of the people she helped were ever caught! Harriet, known as "Moses" Tubman, was a very brave woman who is remembered for her courage and willingness to put her own life in danger to help others.

**Frederick Douglass** was a slave who escaped to freedom as a young man. He became a powerful speaker and author who fought for abolition and women's rights. Douglass wrote *My Bondage and My Freedom,* an autobiography of his life as a former slave.

Famous
African-
Americans

**Benjamin Banneker** was an African-American astronomer, mathematician, surveyor, and almanac writer. He helped determine the District of Columbia's boundaries after Maryland donated land for it to become the national capital.

**Cathy Hughes** and her son, Alfred Liggins III of Lanham, run Radio One which is the largest radio company which directs its programming to urban and African-American listeners. Radio One currently has more than 50 stations in many of the largest African-American markets in the country.

## DID SOMEONE SAY BOO?

# The Ghost of Mary Stewart of White House Farm

Early in the 1800s, a young girl named Mary Stewart, who lived with her family at White House Farm in Chestertown, fell madly in love with a young man. The couple decided to elope late one frosty January night. As Mary was leaving to meet her husband-to-be, the horse she was riding bucked and threw her to the ground. Mary was killed when her head hit a large rock. She had not even ridden past the farm.

Ghosts

According to local legend, the ghost of Mary Stewart has haunted White House Farm ever since. The stone is still there and has a bloodstain, which to this day cannot be cleaned or covered!

DO YOU

BELIEVE IN GHOSTS?

# Sports Stuff

George Herman "Babe" Ruth—one of professional baseball's greatest players; set records for home runs, runs batted in, and pitching; had a lifetime batting average of .342; one of first five Baseball Hall of Famers

Cal Ripken, Jr.—another of professional baseball's greatest players; played a record-setting 2,632 consecutive games; has played entire career for his hometown team—the Baltimore Orioles; voted to the starting lineup of the annual All Star Game a record 15 straight times

Johnny Unitas—professional football player; famous quarterback for championship Baltimore Colts

Sugar Ray Leonard—professional boxer

Sports Stuff

Brooks Robinson and Frank Robinson—professional baseball Hall of Famers; played for Baltimore Orioles

Dominique Dawes—gymnast, Olympic gold medalist known for her grace and power

Gao Chang—gold medalist in women's singles at 1999 Pan American Games

Maryland Jockey Club—America's oldest racing association

# Performing Arts

**Eubie Blake**—musician and composer who wrote ragtime music; awarded the Presidential Medal of Freedom

**Edwin Thomas Booth**—actor; considered one of the finest actors of his day

**John Wilkes Booth**—actor; assassin of President Abraham Lincoln

**"Mama" Cass Elliot**—singer, lead vocalist of the Mamas and the Papas

**Billie Holiday**—singer; one of the greatest blues vocalists of her day

Performing Arts

**Rosa Ponsell**—opera singer; sang at the Metropolitan Opera in New York

**Francis Xavier Bushman**—actor; appeared in more than 400 silent movies

**??????:** Which Mama above is famous for her vocals in the songs, "Monday, Monday," and "California Dreamin'"?

Answer: "Mama" Cass Elliot

# Authors

• Edgar Allan Poe—**author, poet; wrote about the strange, unusual, supernatural, and the macabre (the really gory stuff)**

• H.L. Mencken—**journalist with the Baltimore *Sun,* author, social critic, literary critic, editor; known as the Bard of Baltimore**

• John Barth—**author; novels set in Maryland are known for their humor; wrote *The Sot-Weed Factor***

• Rachel Carson—**author, environmentalist, professor at University of Maryland; wrote *Silent Spring* about the dangers of pesticides and *The Sea Around Us***

• Upton Sinclair—**author, social reformer; his book, *The Jungle,* helped reform the meat-packing industry**

• Dashiell Hammett—**author; wrote detective novels such as *The Maltese Falcon* and *The Thin Man***

Authors

• Adrienne Rich—**poet; advocate for social and political change; National Book Award winner for *Diving into the Wreck***

• Anne Tyler—**author; wrote the Pulitzer Prize-winning *Breathing Lessons***

• Leon Uris—**author; epic novels include *Exodus, Trinity,* and *Topaz***

• Mason Locke Weems—**author, clergyman, biographer**

Word Definition

**nom de plume:** French for pen name, a fictitious name a writer chooses to write under instead of his/her real name

# Artville

**A. Aubrey Bodine**—landscape and seascape photographer; photo journalist for Baltimore *Sun*

**Eugene Leake**—president of Maryland Institute's College of Art; landscape painter

**Charles Peale**—leading painter in colonial Maryland; founded Peale Museum

**Keith Martin**—painter, also created drawings and collages; his work projects mysterious images

**Reuben Kramer**—sculptor; created portrait sculptures and smaller scale pieces

**Herman Maril**—painter and teacher whose works reflect light, color, and nature

**Joyce Scott**—African-American artist who works in many different media

**Grace Hartigan**—teacher, abstract-expressionist

**Raoul Middleman**—portrait and landscape painter

**Tom Miller**—artist; transforms old furniture into colorful, humorous satires

**Screen painting in Baltimore started more than 75 years ago to give city folks some privacy. It grew into an important form of folk art. Johnny Eck, who lived to be 100, was a well-known screenpainter.**

# Very Important People

**Franklin Buchanan**—naval officer; served during Mexican-American War and Civil War; first superintendent of U.S. Naval Academy

**Peter Cooper**—industrialist; built *Tom Thumb*, America's first steam locomotive for B & O Railroad

**Abel Wolman**—co-founder of chemical process that added chlorine to water to kill deadly microorganisms

**Claire McCardell**—fashion designer; creator of the "American look" for women, created pedal pushers (capris), wraparound dresses, hoods, and spaghetti straps

**Very Important People**

**C.P. McCormick**—spice merchant; changed the way McCormick & Co. was run; treated employees as partners, brought the company into prosperity

**Jim Rouse**—builder, developer; awarded the Medal of Freedom; credited with creating the phrases "shopping mall" and "urban renewal"

**Lillie Carroll Jackson**—President of Baltimore and Maryland branches of the National Association for the Advancement of Colored People (NAACP)

**Juanita Jackson Mitchell**—lawyer; fought for civil rights in the NAACP and in state and local courts

# More VIPs

**Clarence Mitchell, Jr.**—Chief NAACP Washington lobbyist, so influential that he was known as "the 101st senator"

**Johns Hopkins**—businessman, banker, philanthropist, founder of Johns Hopkins Hospital and Johns Hopkins University

**Clara Barton**—founder of American Red Cross; served as a nurse during the Civil War and earned the nickname "The Angel of the Battlefield"

**Jacob Blaustein**—founder of the American Oil Co. (Amoco); developed the drive-through filling station and metered pumps

**Helen Taussig**—developed operation to repair heart defects and save the lives of "blue babies" whose blood was starved of oxygen

More VIPs

**Daniel Coit Gilman**—professor, first president of Johns Hopkins University

**William Stewart Halsted**—completed first successful blood transfusion in the U.S.; established first school of surgery in the nation

**Enoch Pratt**—businessman, industrialist; donated funds for Baltimore's Enoch Pratt Free Library

# Pirates!

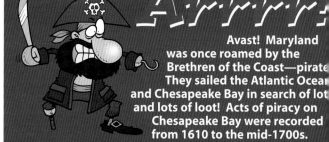

Avast! Maryland was once roamed by the Brethren of the Coast—pirate They sailed the Atlantic Ocean and Chesapeake Bay in search of lot and lots of loot! Acts of piracy on Chesapeake Bay were recorded from 1610 to the mid-1700s.

Blackbeard was said to be the "Fiercest Pirate o Them All!" His black beard was separated into tails and tied with colorful ribbons. Sometimes, he wore flaming sulphur candles in his beard. Blackbeard struck so much fear in the hearts of his enemies the often surrendered just at the sight of him!

In 1718, the governor of Virginia sent a warship commanded by Lieutenant Maynard i search of Blackbeard. Lieutenant Maynard found Blackbeard off the coast of North Carolina. They fought, and before Blackbeard fe he was shot five times and had 20 sword wounds. H head was cut off and stuck on a pole at the mouth o the Hampton River to warn other pirates to stay awa The spot became known as Blackbeard's Point.

The Golden Age of Piracy was drawing to a close. But what about all that buried treasure that no one found? Keep digging!

# Political Leaders

Spiro Agnew—governor, vice president of the U.S.

Charles Carroll—signer of Declaration of Independence; one of Maryland's first U.S. senators

Thurgood Marshall—lawyer, jurist; first African-American associate justice of the U.S. Supreme Court; received NAACP's Spingarn Medal

Albert C. Ritchie—governor for four terms; modernized Maryland state government

Reverdy Johnson—U.S. senator, U.S. attorney general; encouraged Maryland to remain in the Union during Civil War

William Pinkney—statesman, U.S. attorney general, U.S. representative, U.S. senator

John Hanson—member of Continental Congress; first president of the Congress of Confederation

Political Leaders

Barbara Mikulski—first female U.S. senator from Maryland

William Schaefer—received national recognition for his role in bringing new life to Baltimore as mayor

Roger Taney—jurist, U.S. attorney general, U.S. secretary of the treasury, chief justice of U.S. Supreme Court; helped establish Democratic party

# Keeping the Faith

**Naval Academy Chapel, Annapolis**—located at the U.S. Naval Academy; beneath the chapel is a crypt containing the remains of American Revolutionary War naval leader, John Paul Jones

**Old Trinity Church, St. Mary's City**—built in 1829 with bricks salvaged from the State House ruins

**Old Wye Church, Wye Mills**—built in 1721 and later restored; contains a slave gallery, hanging pulpit, and box pews

**Basilica of the Assumption, Baltimore**—first Roman Catholic cathedral in the United States

**Lloyd Street Synagogue, Baltimore**—built in 1845, first synagogue in the state and one of the oldest in the country

**Trinity Chapel, Frederick**—built in 1763, its clock's works have been removed and placed in the Smithsonian

## SCHOOLS

**Washington College, Chestertown**—established in 1782 and named for George Washington

**Johns Hopkins University, Baltimore**—opened in 1876

**St. John's College** (originally King William's School), **Annapolis**—chartered in 1784, known for its nonelective academic program

**Morgan State University, Baltimore**—tradition of serving the African-American community

**United States Naval Academy, Annapolis**

# Historic Sites

**Maryland State House, Annapolis**—begun in 1772, oldest state capitol still in use; only state house to have served as the nation's capitol

**Wye Mill, Wye Mills**—grist mill built in the early 1700s; provided flour to Washington's troops during the Revolution

**Federal Street, Snow Hill**—row of beautiful, historic houses

**Shot Tower, Baltimore**—built in 1828, 215-foot (65.5-meter) tall tower; during the 1800s it was a leading producer of lead shotgun pellets for hunters and the military

**Babe Ruth Birthplace, Baltimore**

**Old South Mountain Inn, near Boonsboro**—stone structure built in 1730, still functions as a restaurant

**Chesapeake & Ohio Canal National Historical Park, Cumberland**

**Antietam National Cemetery, Sharpsburg**—4,776 Federal soldiers are buried here

**Rose Hill Cemetery, Hagerstown**—burial place of some 2,000 Confederate soldiers

**Clara Barton National Historic Site, Glen Echo**

**Jersey Toll House, near Havre de Grace**—built around 1818 to collect tolls for the crossing of a bridge over the Susquehanna River

Historic Sites

Westminster Church and Burying Ground is the burial place of Edgar Allan Poe and other important figures in the city's and country's history.

# Home, Sweet Home!

## Early Residency

**Hammond-Harwood House, Annapolis**—built from 1774–1776, one of the finest Colonial houses in the country

**Edgar Allan Poe House and Museum, Baltimore**

**Homewood, Baltimore**—Charles Carroll, one of the signers of the Declaration of Independence, gave this beautiful country estate to his son as a wedding present

**Barbara Fritchie House and Museum, Frederick**—home of the 95-year-old woman who stood at her door to wave the American flag while Confederate troops marched past

**Kennedy Farmhouse, Samples Manor**—location from which the famous abolitionist John Brown set out on his famous raid on Harper's Ferry in 1859

Home, Sweet Home!

**Teackle Mansion, Princess Anne**—built in the early 1800s

**Beckford, Princess Anne**—built in the 1760s

**Widehall, Chestertown**—built in the 1760s, residents here staged their own Tea Party in May of 1774

# Forts and Battles

## A few of Maryland's famous Forts

● **Fort Frederick, near Indian Springs**—stone fortress built in 1756 to protect the Maryland frontier from French and Indian attacks

● **Fort McHenry, Baltimore**—completed in 1803

● **Fort Washington, on the Potomac River**—built in 1824 to guard the Potomac River; surrounded by a dry moat and entered by a drawbridge

## A few of Maryland's famous Battles

● **Battle of North Point**—War of 1812 battle, occurred after the British had burned Washington, D.C., including the White House

● **Battle of Bladensburg, Prince George's County**—War of 1812 battle

● **Battle of Antietam, Sharpsburg**—bloodiest single day of battle in the Civil War

● **Battle of the Monocacy, near Washington, D.C.**—Civil War battle

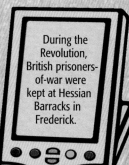

During the Revolution, British prisoners-of-war were kept at Hessian Barracks in Frederick.

Forts and Battles

# Libraries

Check out the following special state libraries! (Do you have a library card? Have you worn it out yet?!)

**Enoch Pratt Free Library, Baltimore**—leading public library in the state

**Johns Hopkins University Library, Baltimore**—largest university library in the state

**Morgan State University, Baltimore**—houses a special collection of African-American writings and documents relating to black history

**Maryland State Library, Annapolis**—founded in 1827

**National Library of Medicine, Bethesda**

Libraries

Maryland libraries circulate almost 10 books per resident every year. That makes them fourth in the nation for library book circulation! Keep up the great reading!

# Zoos & Attractions

- **Pimlico Racetrack, Baltimore**—site of the annual Preakness Stakes
- **Ocean City, on the Atlantic Ocean**—popular seaside resort
- **Babe Ruth Birthplace and Baseball Center, Baltimore**—boasts numerous exhibits and films about the famous sports figure
- **National Aquarium, Baltimore**—12 major themed exhibits, including marine mammals
- **Baltimore Zoo**—nation's third oldest zoo
- **Assateague Island National Seashore**
- **Chesapeake Biological Laboratory, Solomons Island**—visitors can learn about the bay's ecology and maritime history
- **NASA/Goddard Visitor Center, Greenbelt**
- **USF Constellation, Baltimore**—built in 1797, the first frigate built by the U.S.

Zoos & Attractions

LION

# Museums

**Chesapeake Bay Maritime Museum,** St. Michaels

**U.S. Naval Academy Museum,** Annapolis

**St. Clements Island-Potomac River Museum**

**Baltimore Streetcar Museum**

**Baltimore Maritime Museum**—three 20th-century vessels are moored here

**Fire Museum of Maryland, Lutherville**—contains firefighting equipment from the 1820s to the 1960s

**B & O Railroad Station Museum,** Baltimore

Museums

**Rose Hill Manor Children's Museum,** Frederick

**Boonsboro Museum of History**—displays weapons, Civil War artifacts, and other historical items

**Oxford Museum, Oxford**—contains ship models, engines, tools, and other maritime items

# Monuments

**Macedonian Monument, Annapolis**—original wooden figurehead of a British ship captured by Stephen Decatur in 1812

**Tripoli Monument, Annapolis**—a marble column topped by an eagle that commemorates five officers killed during the Barbary Wars in 1804

**Battle Monument, Baltimore**—built to honor the defenders of Baltimore in the 1814 battle against the British invasion

**Washington Monument, Baltimore**—164 feet (50 meters) high, with a 16-foot-high (5-meter) statue of George Washington on the top

**National Shrine of St. Elizabeth Ann Seton, Emmitsburg**—gravesite of the first American woman to be canonized by the Roman Catholic Church

Monuments

*The Barbary Wars were two wars fought between the U.S. and the Barbary States of North Africa in the early 1800s. The Barbary States wanted the U.S. to pay them to protect U.S. ships from pirates.*

# The Show Must Go On!

Walters Art Gallery, Baltimore

Baltimore Museum of Art

Peale Museum, Baltimore

Maryland Art Place, Baltimore

Baltimore Symphony Orchestra

Vagabond Players, Baltimore

Maryland Museum of African Art, Columbia

Academy of the Arts, Easton

Washington County Museum of Fine Arts, Hagerstown

Ballet Theatre, Annapolis

The Peabody Conservatory of Music opened in 1868 as the Academy of Music. After 1874, it became a popular center of musical activity in the state. It is now a division of the Peabody Institute of Johns Hopkins University.

# SEASHORES

The Eastern Shore is separated from the rest of the state by the Chesapeake Bay. Ocean City has 12 miles (19 kilometers) of beaches. It is Maryland's most popular summer resort.

The Assateague Island National Seashore is made up of Assateague Island and several other smaller barrier islands. The islands are a refuge for shorebirds.

# LIGHTHOUSES

Drum Point Lighthouse, near Solomons, is a hexagonal lighthouse, no longer in use. Sandy Point Lighthouse, in the Chesapeake Bay, is a caisson base lighthouse. It was built by hauling a cylinder to its chosen spot, driving the cylinder into place, and filling it with concrete to serve as a base for a house and light.

Concord Point Lighthouse, in Havre de Grace, is the oldest continuously operated lighthouse in the state.

Seashores & Lighthouses

*According to legend, ponies from a 17th-century shipwreck swam to safety on the shore of Assateague Island. The island's resident wild ponies are supposedly descendants of those shipwrecked ponies.*

# Roads, Bridges & Canals

## Roads...

Old National Highway, from Boonsboro, Maryland to Fort Necessity, Pennsylvania

Eastern Shore Highway, along the Chesapeake Bay from Chesapeake City to Tilghman Island

## Bridges

Loy's Station Bridge, near Thurmont—covered bridge

Roddy Road Covered Bridge, near Thurmont

Burnside Bridge, Sharpsburg—where a Northern corps was held off by a few hundred Georgia riflemen near the Antietam battlesite

Chesapeake Bay Bridge, near Annapolis—the Eastern Shore and Western Shore are linked by the double spans of this bridge

Francis Scott Key Bridge, Baltimore—at 1,200 feet (364 meters) long, it is the second longest continuous truss bridge in the nation

**Roads Bridges & Canals**

## Canals

Chesapeake and Delaware Canal, Delaware Bay—handles more traffic each year than the Panama Canal

# Swamps and Caves

## SWAMPS

The Great Pocomoke Swamp, in the eastern part of Maryland, has a large number of bald cypress trees.

The Cranesville Sub-Arctic Swamp, near Oakland, contains many different species of plants usually found in the Arctic. The swamp is designated a National Natural History Landmark.

Hey! Any luck yet?

Swamps and Caves

## CAVES

Crystal Grottoes Caverns, near Boonsboro, boast interesting rock formations and peaceful river surroundings.

A spelunker is a person who explores caves as a hobby.

# Animals of Maryland

Chipmunk
Cottontail
Gray Squirrel
Mink
Muskrat
Opossum
Otter
Raccoon
Red Fox
Skunk
White-tailed Deer
Woodchuck

Animals

# Take a Walk on the Wild Side

Loggerhead Sea Turtle

Peregrine Falcon

Piping Plover

*Indiana Bat*

*Kemp's Turtle*

*Leatherback Sea Turtle*

*Bald Eagle*

Wildlife Watch

*Delmarva Peninsula Fox Squirrel*

*Green Sea Turtle*

79

# Birds

## MARYLAND'S MARVELOUS BIRDS!

BLUE JAY
CANADA GOOSE
CANVASBACK
CARDINAL
GREAT BLUE HERON
MALLARD
MEADOWLARK
MOCKINGBIRD
ORIOLE

PHEASANT
QUAIL
ROBIN
RUFFED GROUSE
SNOW GOOSE
SPARROW
SWALLOW
WARBLER
WOOD DUCK
WREN

The marshes of the Chesapeake Bay area have numerous migratory and resident waterfowl. These marshes are located in the Atlantic Flyway.

Birds

# Insects

## Don't let these Maryland bugs bug you!

Ant
Beetle
Bumblebee
Butterfly
Cicada
Cricket
Dragonfly
Firefly
Grasshopper
Honeybee
Katydid
Ladybug
Mayfly
Mosquito
Moth
Praying Mantis
Termite
Walking Stick
Weevil

Dragonfly

Butterfly

Bumblebee

Ladybug

After hatching, a cicada nymph burrows into the soil. It lives there for as long as 17 years!

Insects

# Fish

Striped Bass
(Rockfish)

White Perch

Shad

Menhaden

Flounder

Black Bass

Trout

River Herring

Sunfish

Marlin

Fish

# Sea Critters

**IN MARYLAND'S SEAS, YOU MAY FIND:**

- Blue Crabs
- Clams
- Dolphin
- Eel
- Jellyfish
- Manatee
- Manta Ray
- Oysters
- Shark
- Skate
- Squid
- Turtle
- Whale

The manatee and the elephant are related! They are both herbivores (plant-eaters) and both have tough skin! Do you think the manatee might like peanuts too?!

Sea Critters

# Seashells

## She sells seashells by the seashore!

| | |
|---|---|
| Auger Shell | Helmet Shell |
| Bubble Shell | Moon Shell |
| Cerith | Mussel |
| Cockle | Oyster |
| Coquina | Periwinkle |

One kind of vampire snail sucks the blood of sharks while the shark is sleeping on the bottom of the sea!

Slipper Shell
Sundial Shell
Tusk Shell
Vampire Shell
Wentletrap
Whelk

# Trees

Ash
Beech
Cedar
Chestnut
Elm
Hemlock
Hickory
Maple
Oak
Poplar
Red Gum
Spruce
Tupelo
White Pine

Trees

# Flowers

## Are you crazy about these Maryland wildflowers?

| | |
|---|---|
| Mayapple | Violet |
| Mountain Laurel | Wild Geranium |
| Jewelweed | Jack-in-the-Pulpit |
| Cranesbill | Spring Beauty |
| Golden Aster | Jacob's Ladder |
| Goldenrod | Buttercup |
| Black-eyed Susan | Chicory |

Flowers

Thousands of years ago, ancient Egyptians made a drink from roasted chicory roots.

Sounds delicious!

# Cream of the Crops

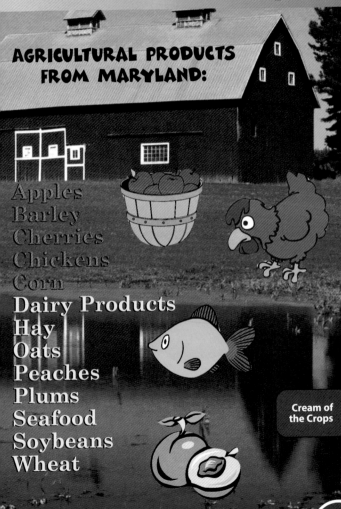

**AGRICULTURAL PRODUCTS FROM MARYLAND:**

Apples
Barley
Cherries
Chickens
Corn
**Dairy Products**
Hay
Oats
Peaches
Plums
Seafood
Soybeans
Wheat

Cream of the Crops

# Maryland Trivia

## Believe it, or not!

Camp David, the official presidential retreat, is located on Catoctin Mountain, overlooking the town of Thurmont, Maryland.

Mount Airy is unique because two counties, Carroll and Frederick, divide it.

Annapolis is known as the sailing capital of the world.

The first dental school in the United States opened at the University of Maryland.

Havre de Grace is known as the decoy capital of the world.

A U.S. flag has flown continuously over Francis Scott Key's birthplace since May 30, 1949.

# Festivals

*Maryland Day, St. Mary's*

*Maryland Hunt Cup, Baltimore*

*Preakness Stakes, Baltimore*

**Fine Arts Festival, Columbia**

**Bay Country Music Festival, Centreville**

**Maryland State Fair, Timonium**

**Maryland Renaissance Festival, Crownsville**

*Olde Princess Anne Days, Somerset County*

*Candlelight Tour of Historic Havre de Grace*

# Holidays

## Calendar

| | | |
|---|---|---|
| Martin Luther King, Jr. Day, *3rd Monday in January* | Presidents' Day, *3rd Monday in February* | St. Patrick's Day, *March 17* |
| Memorial Day, *last Monday in May*  | Flag Day, *June 14* | Independence Day, *July 4*  |
| Defenders Day, *September 12* | Columbus Day, *2nd Monday in October* | Veterans Day, *November 11* |
|  | Thanksgiving, *4th Thursday in November* | Christmas, *December 25*  |

**Baltimore holds a Turtle Derby in July!**

# Famous Food

Apple Pie
Batter-fried Stuffed
Hard Crab
Cheesecake
Clams Casino
Crab Cakes
Crab Soup
Maryland Tomatoes

Oysters
Pan-seared Sea Bass
Rice Pudding
Seafood Imperial
Shrimp Cocktail
Soft-shelled Crabs
Steamed Blue Crabs

Yumm, yumm. This is great!

Let's dig in!

## MARYLAND WORKS!

The federal government is the most important employer in the state. Many Marylanders work in government agencies and on military bases. Food processing is an important state industry. Food processing activities include the production of dairy  products, meat products, beverages, fruit and vegetable products, and seafood. Service industries, like health care and education, offer services to groups or individuals. Maryland is also known for its manufactured goods. Electrical machinery and equipment are important manufactured goods, as well as chemicals and chemical products.

Growing types of manufacturing in the state include printing and publishing, electronics, and medical and scientific equipment.

**Business & Trade**

Baltimore is the state's leading wholesale and retail trade center. It is served by various shipping lines and trucking companies, as well as major railroads. Several other trade centers exist in other parts of the state.

# State Books & Websites

*America the Beautiful: Maryland* by Deborah Kent

*Let's Discover the States: Mid-Atlantic* by the Aylesworths

*My First Book about Maryland* by Carole Marsh

*Maryland Jeopardy* by Carole Marsh

*The Maryland Experience Series* by Carole Marsh

## COOL MARYLAND WEBSITES

www.marylandexperience.com

www.50states.com

www.state.md.us

www.mdarchives.state.md.us

# Maryland
## Glossary

**bay**: a part of a sea or lake that cuts into a coastline to form a hollow curve

**colony**: a region controlled by a distant country

**immigrant**: a person who comes to a new country to live

**jockey**: a person whose work is riding horses in races

**jousting**: a sport where players on horseback have 8 seconds to use lances to "spear" rings for points

**port**: a harbor where ships can load and unload

**revolution**: the overthrow of a government

**skipjack**: a type of sailboat used for dredging oysters from the ocean

**secede**: to voluntarily give up being part of an organized group

**tradition**: a custom handed down from the past

# Maryland
## Spelling Bee

Here are some special Maryland-related words to learn! To take the Spelling Bee, have someone call out the words and you spell them aloud or write them on a piece of paper.

*SPELLING WORDS*

| | |
|---|---|
| Annapolis | lacrosse |
| Appalachian | Patapsco |
| Assateague | Patuxent |
| Baltimore | Pocomoke |
| Chesapeake | Preakness |
| Choptank | Nanticoke |
| Delmarva | Sassafras |
| Frederick | Susquehanna |
| jousting | |

# About the Author

## ABOUT THE AUTHOR...

CAROLE MARSH has been writing about Maryland for more than 20 years. She is the author of the popular Maryland State Stuff series for young readers and creator, along with her son, Michael Marsh, of "Maryland Facts and Factivities," a CD-ROM widely used in Maryland schools. The author of more than 100 Maryland books and other supplementary educational materials on the state, Marsh is currently working on a new collection of Maryland materials for young people. Marsh correlates her Maryland materials to the Maryland Content Standards for Social Studies. Many of her books and other materials have been inspired by or requested by Maryland teachers and librarians.

## EDITORIAL ASSISTANTS:

### TERRY BRIGGS,

BILLIE WALBURN,

JILL SANDERS

You know... that was a great experience!

Sure was! Thanks for taking me along.